W9-DAN-964

History Highlights

TIMELINE *of the* INDUSTRIAL REVOLUTION

By Charlie Samuels

Gareth Stevens
Publishing

Please visit our Web site www.garethstevens.com. For a free color catalog of all our high-quality books, call toll free 1-800-542-2595 or fax 1-877-542-2596.

Library of Congress Cataloging-in-Publication Data
Samuels, Charlie, 1961-
    A timeline of the Industrial Revolution / Charlie Samuels.
        p. cm. — (History highlights)
    Includes index.
    ISBN 978-1-4339-3492-6 (library binding)
    ISBN 978-1-4339-3493-3 (pbk.)
    ISBN 978-1-4339-3494-0 (6-pack)
    1. Industrialization—History—Juvenile literature. 2. Industrial revolution—Juvenile literature. I. Title.
HD2329.S24 2010
330.9'034—dc22   2009042094

Published in 2010 by
Gareth Stevens Publishing
111 East 14th Street, Suite 349
New York, NY 10003

© 2010 The Brown Reference Group Ltd.

For Gareth Stevens Publishing:
Art Direction: Haley Harasymiw
Editorial Direction: Kerri O'Donnell

For The Brown Reference Group Ltd:
Editorial Director: Lindsey Lowe
Managing Editor: Tim Cooke
Editor: Ben Hollingum
Children's Publisher: Anne O'Daly
Design Manager: David Poole
Designer: Karen Perry
Picture Manager: Sophie Mortimer
Production Director: Alastair Gourlay

Picture Credits:
Front Cover: Mary Evans Picture Library

Corbis: W. A. Raymondk: 17; istockphoto: 7b, 29bl; Henrick: 36; Hulton Archive; 8, 14; Timeflight: 35; Jupiter Images: Photos.com: 5, 9, 11b, 13, 15t, 16, 18, 19, 23b, 25, 26, 27i, 29t , 30-31, 31 b, 32, 33, 34b, 37, 38b, 39b, 40, 41, 43, 44, 45t; Stockxpert: 7t, 10, 11t, 15b, 21, 22, 34t, 42, 45b; Shutterstock: Concettina D' Agnese

All Artworks Brown Reference Group

Publisher's note to educators and parents: Our editors have carefully reviewed the Web sites that appear on p. 47 to ensure that they are suitable for students. Many Web sites change frequently, however, and we cannot guarantee that a site's future contents will continue to meet our high standards of quality and educational value. Be advised that students should be closely supervised whenever they access the Internet.

Manufactured in the United States of America
1 2 3 4 5 6 7 8 9 12 11 10

CPSIA compliance information: Batch #BRW0102GS: For further information contact Gareth Stevens, New York, New York at 1-800-542-2595.

Contents

Introduction 4

The Enlightenment 6

Textile Machines 10

Farm Machinery 14

Canal Transportation 18

The Industrial Revolution 22

The Beginning of Railroads 28

The Great Exhibition 32

Germs and Disease 36

The Age of Invention 40

Glossary 46

Further Reading 47

Index 48

Introduction

From 1700 to 1900, industrialization swept western Europe and North America. The change was so rapid that the period became known as the Industrial Revolution.

The process began with the so-called Age of Reason, when Europe's thinkers began to approach the natural world in a systematic way. They made close observations of substances and phenomena; they tested their theories with experiments; and they recorded their findings accurately. As knowledge grew, some individuals brought together theory and practice. They explored new sources of energy or produced new machines that made it easier to manufacture or transport goods. The textile industry led the way, followed by agriculture, transportation, and iron and steel. Breakthroughs such as the steam engine changed the way that people worked and traveled.

A Social Revolution

The growth of industry produced changes throughout society. Machines were housed in factories and mills, so workers moved to be near them. Industrial towns and cities grew rapidly. Mass-production meant that more people could buy more possessions, marking the start of a more consumer-oriented society. Railroads and steamships enabled people to travel farther and more quickly than had been imaginable. At the end of the nineteenth century, the invention of the internal combustion engine and the radio looked forward to the modern age.

About This Book

This book focuses on two centuries of technological advances, from 1700 to 1900. It contains two different types of timelines. Along the bottom of the pages is a timeline that covers the whole period. It lists key events and developments, color-coded by region. Each chapter also has its own timeline, running vertically down the sides of the pages. This timeline provides more specific details about the particular subject of the chapter.

Spools of yarn on a weaving machine. The mechanization of textile manufacturing marked the beginning of the Industrial Revolution. ↓

The Enlightenment

The Enlightenment was a philosophical movement that influenced European society and culture in the eighteenth century, a period known as the Age of Reason.

Frederick the Great of Prussia was a leading "enlightened monarch." →

TIMELINE
1700–1710

1701 In the War of the Spanish Succession, the Grand Alliance (England, the Netherlands, the Holy Roman Empire, and German states) fights against France.

1702 The first English language daily newspaper opens in England.

1703 In Japan, a huge earthquake devastates Tokyo, then known as Edo.

1700　　　　1702　　　　1704

1701 Yale College is set up in New Haven, Connecticut.

1702 French and English colonies in North America begin Queen Anne's War.

1704 The Grand Alliance wins the Battle of Blenheim.

KEY:

Europe

Americas

Asia, Africa, and Oceania

Many thinkers were horrified by the conflict that religion had caused in recent centuries. They looked for other ways for people to find meaning in their lives. In *An Essay Concerning Human Understanding* (1690), the English philosopher John Locke stated a key principle of the new thinking. He argued that people were not naturally evil but could be made so by circumstances.

↑ The Prussian palace of Sans Souci provided a refuge for French writer Voltaire.

Deism

Some thinkers rejected religion outright. Others claimed a more personal relationship with God than through organized churches. This "deist" view suggested that God was kind but distant. He had given humans the capacity for reason and empowered them to control their own fate.

Timeline of the Enlightenment

1730 English deist Matthew Tyndale attacks the supernatural element of organized religion.

1734 Voltaire publishes his *Lettres philosophiques*, which call for political and religious toleration.

1735 Swedish botanist Carolus Linnaeus sets out his system of plant classification.

1736 Laws against witchcraft are repealed in England.

1740 Frederick II ("the Great") of Prussia ascends to the throne; he introduces economic, legal, and social reforms.

1747 Diderot and d'Alembert begin their work on the *Encyclopedia*. The first volume is published four years later.

⇐ Carolus Linnaeus's system of classifying plants and animals is still used today.

1706 The Spanish found the settlement of Albuquerque, New Mexico.

1707 The death of Emperor Aurangzeb sends the Delhi sultanate into steep decline.

1709 In the Great Northern War, Russia wins a decisive victory over Sweden in the Battle of Poltava.

1706

1708

1710

1707 The Act of Union joins England and Scotland together to form the United Kingdom of Great Britain.

1709 Alliance forces defeat the French in the Battle of Malplaquet, but with heavy losses.

Timeline (continued)

1750 Voltaire goes into exile in Germany.

1755 Dr. Samuel Johnson produces his *Dictionary of the English Language.*

1764 Italian legal theorist Cesare Beccaria advocates reform of prisons and abolition of torture.

1766 Catherine the Great grants freedom of worship to Russians.

1776 Bavarian lawyer Adam Weisshaupt founds the Order of Illuminati, a cult dedicated to spreading a new religion based on reason.

Voltaire's writings about society earned him harsh criticism. ⇒

SPAIN country using Enlightenment ideas in state reform
■ scientific society with date of establishment
○ observatory

St. Petersburg 1724
Uppsala 1710
Stockholm 1741
SWEDEN
Vänern
Vättern
DENMARK–NORWAY
Baltic Sea
North Sea
Copenhagen 1742
Edinburgh 1739
Dublin 1731
PRUSSIA
Berlin 1700
Elbe
Birmingham 1766
Haarlem 1752
Göttingen 1736
London 1660
Rotterdam 1773
Vistula
Rouen 1736
Amiens 1750
Rhine
Caen 1705
Reims 1776
Mannheim 1755
Paris 1666
Nancy 1736
BAVARIA
Orléans 1753
Dijon 1723
Munich 1759
Danube
ATLANTIC OCEAN
FRANCE
Geneva 1776
AUSTRIAN EMPIRE
Clermont-Ferrand 1705
Lyon 1700
MILAN
Padua 1779
Bordeaux 1712
Marseille 1726
PARMA
Florence 1752
Toulouse 1782
TUSCANY
Ebro
Corsica
Naples 1779
PORTUGAL
Madrid 1713
SPAIN
Balearic Islands
SARDINIA
Lisbon 1779
Guadiana
Sardinia
Mediterranean Sea
0 600 km
0 400 mi

⇐ Enlightenment ideas spread across Europe, promoting scientific research and political reform.

The rise of natural sciences had discredited traditional explanations of the universe. Instead, thinkers used close observation and experiment to study the world around them. This method is known as empiricism. The English scientist Isaac Newton embodied the new approach.

Social Reform

Along with the challenge to established religion came a demand for social change. French philosophers such as

TIMELINE 1710–1720

1711 With British help, New England colonists take Acadia in Canada from the French.

1713 At the end of the War of the Spanish Succession, France's favored candidate, Philip V, becomes king of Spain.

1714 After the death of Queen Anne, King George I begins the Hanoverian dynasty in Britain.

1710   1712   1714

1713 The Peace of Utrecht ends Queen Anne's War. France surrenders American territory to Britain.

1714 The Ottoman Empire goes to war against Venice and the Holy Roman Empire.

KEY:

Europe

Americas

Asia, Africa, and Oceania

Montesquieu, Voltaire, and Rousseau advocated civil liberties such as equality before the law and free speech. They argued that such liberties could be the basis of a "social contract" between ruler and people.

Many monarchs felt threatened by the new ideas; Voltaire himself was jailed and forced into exile. Yet some of Europe's rulers, notably Catherine the Great of Russia, Joseph II of Austria, and Prussia's King Frederick II, adopted the new ideas. They began social and legal reforms. Even so, these "enlightened despots" stopped short of introducing democracy.

Near the end of the 18th century, the American and French revolutions adopted many key beliefs of the Enlightenment. Yet in France, the optimism of the Age of Reason gave way to the Reign of Terror, plunging the continent into a new cycle of turmoil.

The *Encyclopedia* had many illustrations of technical processes. ⟫

The *Encyclopedia*

Philosopher Denis Diderot and mathematician Jean d'Alembert set out to produce a compendium of contemporary knowledge. Its 33 volumes were published over 26 years. They contained articles by leading French thinkers. The articles treated practical subjects such as baking alongside radical topics such as progressive philosophical ideas and political liberalism.

1715 Settlers push west into the foothills of eastern Appalachia.

1717 The Viceroyalty of New Grenada is created by Colombia, Ecuador, Venezuela, and Panama.

1719 English author Daniel Defoe writes *Robinson Crusoe*, a novel based on the real-life desert-island experiences of marooned sailor Alexander Selkirk

1716   1718   1720

1715 In Scotland, the Jacobite uprising tries unsuccessfully to put James Edward Stuart on the British throne.

1718 The Ottoman Empire begins the Tulip Period, a time of cultural renewal.

Textile Machines

After centuries of spinning fibers by hand, the textile industry was totally mechanized within a period of 70 years. Textile machinery led the Industrial Revolution.

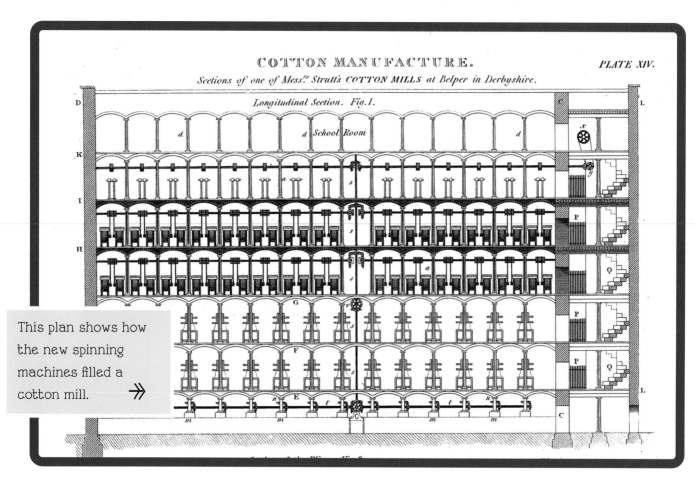

COTTON MANUFACTURE.   PLATE XIV.

Sections of one of Messⁿ Strutt's COTTON MILLS at Belper in Derbyshire.

Longitudinal Section. Fig.1.

This plan shows how the new spinning machines filled a cotton mill. →

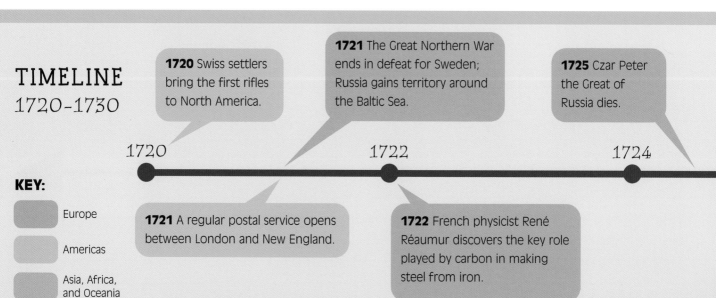

TIMELINE
1720–1730

1720 Swiss settlers bring the first rifles to North America.

1721 The Great Northern War ends in defeat for Sweden; Russia gains territory around the Baltic Sea.

1725 Czar Peter the Great of Russia dies.

1720   1722   1724

1721 A regular postal service opens between London and New England.

1722 French physicist René Réaumur discovers the key role played by carbon in making steel from iron.

KEY:

Europe

Americas

Asia, Africa, and Oceania

The first aid to spinning was the distaff, a long stick onto which wool was wound from about 5500 B.C. The spinner held the distaff under her arm and teased out a long strand of wool, which she spun between the fingers of the other hand. The spun thread wound itself around a rotating spindle.

The spinning wheel was used in Europe from the 1200s. It used a large vertical wheel. A belt drive turned the spindle, while the spinner pulled wool from a vertical distaff. A foot treadle was added to turn the wheel in the sixteenth century.

≪ The spinning wheel was used from the 1200s.

Great Advances

Two major advances came in England in the eighteenth century. James Hargreaves invented

Timeline of Textile Machinery

1200s The spinning wheel is used in Europe.

1733 John Kay invents the flying shuttle.

1764 James Hargreaves invents the spinning jenny.

1769 Richard Arkwright pioneers the spinning frame.

1779 Samuel Crompton invents the spinning mule.

1785 The steam-powered loom is invented by Edmund Cartwright.

1828 John Thorpe invents the ring-spinning mule.

≪ Spinning was seen as "women's work" even after the process was mechanized.

1726 Irish writer Jonathan Swift writes his satire *Gulliver's Travels.*

1727 Quakers call for the abolition of the transatlantic slave trade.

1729 The city of Baltimore is founded as a center for shipbuilding.

1726

1728

1730

1727 Coffee is grown for the first time in Brazil; it will become the country's main export.

1728 Danish navigator Vitus Bering sails through the strait between Siberia and Alaska; today it is known as the Bering Strait.

1729 The German composer Johann Sebastian Bach writes the *St. Matthew Passion.*

The Loom

A loom is a frame to hold parallel warp (lengthwise) threads. The weft (crosswise) thread is wound on a shuttle, which the weaver works in and out of the warp threads. Another frame called a heddle holds sets of wires ending in rings through which the warp threads move. Controlled by treadles, the heddle lifts warp threads to create different kinds of weave.

The loom was gradually developed to make weaving easier. →

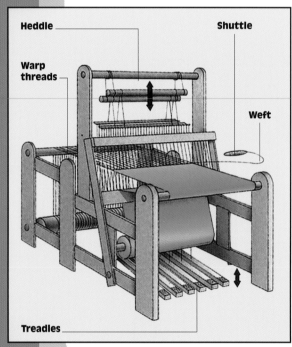

Heddle

Warp threads

Shuttle

Weft

Treadles

the spinning jenny in 1764 and Richard Arkwright invented the spinning frame in 1769. The jenny produced woolen yarn. The spinning frame was powered by a waterwheel and made cotton yarn for weaving. The two ideas were brought together in 1779 by the spinning mule. The mule produced 48 strands of fine yarn at the same time.

In principle, the machines are much the same. The textile fibers are wound onto rotating spindles that move on a frame. The frame first pulls the strands outward, twisting them to form yarn; it then moves back while the yarn is wound onto bobbins.

The Story of Weaving

Having produced the yarn, the weaver then has to make it into cloth. This is the job of a loom. At its simplest, it is a frame that holds a set of parallel threads called the warp. The weaver interweaves them at right angles with another thread—the weft—that is carried on a bobbin in a boat-shaped holder known as a shuttle. The first improvement was the addition

TIMELINE 1730–1740

1733 English inventor John Kay patents the flying shuttle loom, opening the way to the industrialization of cotton production.

1735 The Swedish botanist known by the Latin name Carolus Linnaeus sets out his system for classifying plants.

1730   1732   1734

1731 Benjamin Franklin opens the first subscription library in North America.

1734 French writer Voltaire publishes his *Philosophical Letters*, calling for political and religious toleration.

KEY:

Europe

Americas

Asia, Africa, and Oceania

↑ New Lanark in Scotland was planned for mill workers to live nearby.

Weavers

Before the Industrial Revolution, weaving was a cottage industry. Workers wove on looms at home. The new weaving machines made it more convenient to bring workers together in a single place: a factory. Now a few people could oversee a number of mechanized looms.

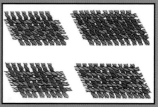

↑ A loom produces different weaves depending on the different warp threads lifted by the heddle.

of cords that pulled up every other warp thread to make it easier to pass the shuttle from side to side. Soon weavers added treadles to work the cords.

Weaving sped up greatly in 1733 when English engineer John Kay invented the flying shuttle, a mechanism that enables the weaver to "throw" the shuttle rapidly from side to side. Mechanized looms came next. At first, they were driven by water power, but that changed in 1785. In that year, English inventor Edmund Cartwright made the first steam-powered loom; soon most looms were driven by steam engines.

1735 In England, John Harrison builds the first marine chronometer; it keeps accurate time at sea, making navigation more precise.

1738 Swiss mathematician Daniel Bernoulli formulates theories about how liquids flow.

1739 French explorers Paul and Pierre Mallet reach Santa Fe, New Mexico, after traveling west from the Mississippi River.

1736   1738   1740

1735 Briton Abraham Darby uses coke in his blast furnaces to produce iron more efficiently.

1736 England repeals its medieval laws against witchcraft.

1738 French inventor Charles de Labelye invents the caisson, a watertight chamber that allows people to work underwater.

Farm Machinery

After prehistoric times, there was little progress in farming technology until the metal plowshare, which appeared in the West late in the eighteenth century.

This steam plow was imagined in the late 1700s, but in the end was never built. ⇒

TIMELINE
1740–1750

KEY:

Europe

Americas

Asia, Africa, and Oceania

1742 German composer Georg Frederick Handel premieres his oratorio *The Messiah*.

1742 Swedish astronomer Anders Celsius devises the centigrade scale, measuring temperature from 0° to 100°.

1743 Hostilities break out between the Ottoman Empire and Safavid Persia.

1740   1742   1744

1740 Frederick II the Great becomes king of Prussia; Maria Theresa becomes empress of the Hapsburg Empire. They will both be leading "enlightened" rulers.

1742 Coal is first mined in West Virginia.

1745 The Ashanti use firearms for the first time in Africa to defeat the neighboring state of Dagomba.

In 1785, English engineer Robert Ransome invented a cast-iron plowshare. In the United States 12 years later, Charles Newbold also patented a plow with a cast-iron plowshare. Pulled by horses, these plows could cut through the soil more deeply and easily than wooden plows. From 1839, the U.S. industrialist John Deere produced cast-iron plows in large numbers.

By 1862, Dutch farmers were using steam plows. The plows had reversible plowshares mounted in a wheeled frame that was winched from one side of a field to the other by a pair of steam traction engines. Other farmers in Europe and the United States used steam tractors to pull standard plows.

⤒ A drawing from the late 1700s shows a plow, roller, harrow, and seed drill.

Timeline of Farm Machinery

1701 Jethro Tull invents the mechanical seed drill.

1785 The cast-iron plowshare is invented in England.

1819 U.S. engineers pioneer the cast-iron plow.

1834 Cyrus McCormick patents his reaping machine.

1838 The combine harvester is invented.

1878 John Appleby develops a separate binding machine.

1908 The steam caterpillar tractor appears.

⬉ The mechanized seeder was a descendent of Jethro Tull's original seed drill.

1747 Frenchman Denis Diderot begins work on the *Encyclopedia*, which collects contemporary knowledge on a wide range of subjects.

1748 Excavations begin on the site of the rediscovered ancient city of Pompeii, buried under volcanic ash in A.D. 79.

1746   1748   1750

1746 The cities of Lima and Callao in Peru are destroyed by an earthquake that kills 18,000 people.

1748 Platinum is mined for the first time in South America and exported to Europe.

1749 A French force sets out from Canada to claim the Ohio Valley for France.

Tull's Breakthrough

After a farmer had prepared the soil, the next step was to plant the seed. Since ancient times seed had been scattered by hand. This was hard labor, and meant that crops grew wherever the seeds fell. That all changed in 1701, when the English agriculturist Jethro Tull invented the mechanical seed drill. Using the drill, the farmer sowed the seed in parallel rows. That made the crop easier to weed by hoeing and easier to harvest. In turn, that encouraged the mechanization of other parts of the agricultural process.

↑ This early horse-drawn reaper and binder was invented by Cyrus McCormick.

Harvest Machines

After harvesting, crops such as wheat had to be threshed to remove the grain. Threshing by hand was a labor-intensive operation using whiplike flails. In 1786, the process was mechanized when Scottish millwright Andrew Meikle invented the threshing machine.

The last major farming process to be mechanized was reaping. Credit for the key invention usually goes to Cyrus McCormick. In fact, other inventors developed reapers that were better than McCormick's machine. However, McCormick had the business sense to make sure that his reapers were the most popular. Cyrus

TIMELINE
1750–1760

1751 A major victory over the French increases Britain's hold on India.

1754 The world's first iron-rolling mill starts operations in England.

1754 Clashes break out between American frontier settlers and French troops.

1750   1752   1754

1752 Benjamin Franklin investigates the nature of electricity, including his famous experiment of flying a kite in a lightning storm.

1754 At the Albany Congress, Benjamin Franklin's plan to unite the American colonies is rejected by colonial authorities.

KEY:

Europe

Americas

Asia, Africa, and Oceania

made his first reaper in 1831, when he was only 22, and patented a machine in 1834. McCormick reapers were prominent in 1851 at the Great Exhibition in London and at the Paris International Exposition of 1855. In 1879, McCormick created the McCormick Harvesting Machine Company, which made 4,000 machines a year.

Steam and Gas Power

A new phase in mechanization came with the invention of the steam traction engine, the steam caterpillar tractor, and, in 1910, gasoline-driven combine harvesters. At first, a tractor pulled the harvester. Then designers made the motive power part of the machine. By the mid-twentieth century, self-propelled combines were a common sight on the prairies of the Midwest.

Combine Harvester

In the 1830s, after the pioneering work of U.S. inventor John Lane, engineers began to make combine harvesters that cut the wheat and bound it into sheaves. There were also separate binding machines. Later combines also threshed the grain, but were so heavy they needed 10 or more horses to pull them.

← This early combine thresher in Oregon took 30 horses and four men to work.

1756 In India, 145 British prisoners are said to suffocate in the "Black Hole of Calcutta."

1756 Prussia's invasion of Saxony sparks the Seven Years' War.

1759 The construction of the Eddystone Lighthouse in the English Channel uses pioneering techniques that are widely adopted around the world.

1756   1758   1760

1755 The French and Indian War breaks out as British and French settlers and their respective native allies fight for control of North America.

1759 The French thinker Voltaire, in exile for his radical views, publishes his satire *Candide.*

1759 A victory for General James Wolfe over the French at Quebec establishes British supremacy over Canada.

Canal Transportation

At the end of the eighteenth century, the main method of moving heavy goods was by canal. Raw materials and finished goods were towed on barges by horses.

This view from 1819 shows the Grand Junction Canal in England. ⇒

TIMELINE
1760–1770

1762 Russian nobles help Czar Peter III's wife seize power; she becomes Catherine II the Great.

1762 French writer Jean-Jacques Rousseau pubishes *The Social Contract*.

1763 In North America, the Treaty of Paris hands all French territories in Canada and east of the Mississippi to the British, who also gain Florida from Spain.

1760   1762   1764

KEY:

Europe

Americas

Asia, Africa, and Oceania

1760 The start of the shogunate of Ieharu begins a period of economic problems and social unrest in Japan.

1763 The Treaty of Paris ends the Seven Years' War.

1764 The British introduce the Sugar Act, aimed at raising taxes from the American colonies.

Timeline of Canal Transportation

1757 The Sankey Brook Navigation is built near St. Helens, England.

1761 The Bridgewater Canal, designed by James Brindley, opens near Manchester, England.

1779 English engineer William Twiss builds a waterway at Coteau-du-Lac, Quebec.

1819 A canal for ocean-going ships connects the English city of Exeter with the sea.

1822 For the first time, vessels use a canal across Scotland.

1825 The Erie Canal opens to carry grain from the Great Lakes to New York City via the Hudson River.

The Chinese built canals for transportation more than 2,000 years ago. Extensive canal systems were used for drainage and irrigation in northern India around the same time and by the Middle Ages in the Netherlands. Canals for industrial transportation were first used in England in 1757. The Sankey Brook Navigation near St. Helens in northern England included a pair of side-by-side locks known as staircase locks.

The first important canal was the Bridgewater Canal near Manchester, England. It was designed by engineer James Brindley and completed in 1761. It was a contour (gravity-flow) canal with no locks. A canal that takes a more direct route needs locks for coping with inclines,

1765 After protests led by the new Sons of Liberty movement, the British are forced to repeal the Stamp Act, a tax on American legal documents and newspapers.

1768 England's Captain James Cook sets out on his first voyage to the South Pacific.

1769 In America, the Sons (and Daughters) of Liberty urge consumers not to buy British goods.

1766

1768

1770

1767 The Spaniards expel the Jesuits from South America, accusing them of stirring up rebellion among native peoples.

1769 Cook sails around New Zealand and charts the coasts of the two islands.

How a Lock Works

The pound, or chamber, lock encloses a stretch of water so it can be raised or lowered. When a boat approaches a closed lock from upstream, sluices in the upstream gates are opened to fill the lock with water. 1. The gates are opened and the boat enters the lock. 2. The gates are closed. Sluices in the lower gates open so the water level falls to the downstream level. 3. The lower gates open and the boat exits. For a boat traveling in the opposite direction, the sequence is reversed.

tunnels for going through hills, and aqueducts for crossing valleys.

Canals were narrow, so the barges that traveled on them had to be narrower still, although they could be up to 72 feet (22 m) long. They were called narrowboats. They could carry a load of 33 tons

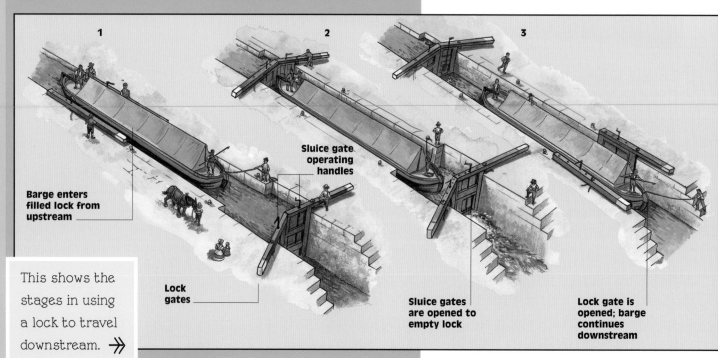

Barge enters filled lock from upstream

Lock gates

Sluice gate operating handles

Sluice gates are opened to empty lock

Lock gate is opened; barge continues downstream

This shows the stages in using a lock to travel downstream. ⇒

TIMELINE
1770–1780

KEY:

Europe

Americas

Asia, Africa, and Oceania

1770   1772   1774

1770 James Cook discovers the east coast of Australia and claims it for Britain.

1773 Prussian scientist Wilhelm Scheele isolates hydrogen and oxygen (his findings are published in 1777).

1775 The Battle of Lexington sees the first shots fired in the American Revolutionary War.

1770 British troops shoot dead five colonials in the Boston Massacre.

1773 James Cook becomes the first navigator to cross the Antarctic Circle in the Southern Ocean.

1775 Frontiersman Daniel Boone marks out the Wilderness Road through the Cumberland Gap to Kentucky.

(30 tonnes), while a wagon could carry just 2.2 tons (2 tonnes).

Other canals soon followed. In 1773, Scottish engineer James Watt surveyed a route in Scotland that would link a series of lochs in order to join the North Sea and the North Atlantic Ocean. Work began in 1803, and the first vessel sailed through the canal in 1822.

Canals in North America

In North America, the first canal with locks was probably a waterway at Coteau-du-Lac, Quebec, built in 1779 to bypass a stretch of rough water on the St. Lawrence River. In 1825, the Erie Canal was completed to carry grain from the Great Lakes to New York City via the Hudson River. Within 10 years, receipts from tolls had repaid the cost of construction. The enlarged modern canal, now part of the New York State canal system, can carry barges of up to 2,204 tons (2,000 tonnes).

The Story of Locks

The pound lock was invented in ancient China. It was perfected in Holland and Italy in about 1370. Its hinged gates close at an angle that faces upstream. That means that the pressure of down-flowing water helps to keep them shut. Sluices in or around the gates can be raised or lowered to let water in or out of the lock.

↑ The technology of locks, like this example in Ireland, has barely changed over 600 years.

1776 The Delcaration of Independence is signed by representatives of the 13 colonies on July 4.

1777 A British army is defeated at the Battle of Saratoga.

1779 Spain also declares war on Britain.

1779 In Britain, the Iron Bridge is built across the Severn River; it is the first structure in the world made entirely from cast iron.

1776

1778

1780

1776 In France, publication is completed of the 28-volume *Encyclopedia*, one of the great works of the Enlightenment.

1778 France declares war on Britain in support of the American cause.

1779 On a third expedition to the Pacific, James Cook is killed in a violent dispute with Hawaiian islanders.

The Industrial Revolution

From around 1750, mechanization and the growth of cities transformed western Europe and North America from agricultural communities to industrial societies.

The world's first iron bridge was built at Coalbrookdale, England, in 1779. →

TIMELINE
1780–1790

1781 German-born British astronomer William Herschel discovers the planet Uranus.

1782 Spanish settlers found Los Angeles.

1783 In France, the Montgolfier brothers make the first flight in their hot-air balloon.

1780

1782

1784

KEY:

Europe

Americas

Asia, Africa, and Oceania

1781 British forces in America surrender at Yorktown, ending the fighting in the American Revolutionary War.

1783 In the Treaty of Paris, Britain formally recognizes the independence of the United States.

1784 The dollar becomes the U.S. monetary unit.

↑ Children move coal in a mine. Child labor was restricted in Britain only in 1833.

The Industrial Revolution began in Britain. Conditions there were ideal. The country had plentiful coal and iron deposits. Businessmen had money to invest. And the British Empire was hungry for exports. The impetus came from textiles. The manufacture of cotton and other fabrics was transformed by the invention of mechanical means of spinning and weaving. The new machines were big and expensive. They needed workers to come together in large mills. Communities changed from making many goods for local consumption to manufacturing a limited range of products for a wider market.

Mechanization also encouraged the growth of heavy

Timeline of the Industrial Revolution

1733 John Kay invents the flying shuttle, which speeds up the weaving process.

1764 Scottish engineer James Watt improves the steam engine by adding a condenser and devises mechanisms that turn linear into circular motion for powering machinery.

1776 Scottish political economist Adam Smith publishes the influential *The Wealth of Nations*.

1815 Scottish engineer John McAdam makes the first paved roads, using crushed stone.

1825 The world's first commercial railroad opens between Stockton and Darlington in England.

← James Watt's changes made the steam engine more useful to industry.

1787 Meeting in Philadelphia, the Constitutional Convention adopts the U.S. Constitution. It is later ratified by all 13 states.

1788 The First Fleet of British settlers, including more than 700 convicts, lands at Botany Bay in Australia.

1789 On July 14, citizens of Paris storm the Bastille prison; the event is usually seen as the start of the French Revolution.

1786

1788

1790

1787 A British antislavery group buys land in Sierra Leone on the west coast of Africa to found a colony for freed slaves.

1788 Britain's *Times* newspaper is first published in London.

1789 George Washington is elected unopposed as the first president of the United States.

Timeline (continued)

1833 Britain's Factory Act restricts the use of children in industry.

1838 Isambard Kingdom Brunel's iron steamship *Great Western* becomes the first vessel to run regular transatlantic passenger services.

1839 U.S. inventor Charles Goodyear discovers how to vulcanize rubber, making the material more durable.

1856 In England, Henry Bessemer produces cheap, carbon-tempered steel from iron ore.

→ The Industrial Revolution's early centers included Britain, Germany, and Belgium.

industry. Early in the eigtheenth century, the English ironmaster Abraham Darby found a way of producing iron on a large scale, using coke in a blast furnace.

Steam Power

Even more important for the huge increase in iron and steel output and in coal extraction later in the century was the replacing of water power by steam power. The principle of the steam engine had been known since around 1700. Beam engines had been built to pump water from mines. But it was only with James Watt's changes to the basic design in the 1760s that steam power came of age.

Watt and his collaborator, the industrialist

major textile or silk producing area 1850
heavy industrial or mining area 1850
borders 1850

0 — 600 km
0 — 400 mi

SWEDEN
NORWAY
Christiania   Stockholm
North Sea
Göteborg   Riga
Glasgow Edinburgh
DENMARK   Baltic Sea   Memel
UNITED KINGDOM   Copenhagen
Manchester Leeds   NETHERLANDS   Danzig   Königsberg
Liverpool Sheffield   Hamburg   GERMAN   RUSSIAN EMPIRE
Birmingham   Amsterdam   STATES   Warsaw
Bristol London   Dortmund   Berlin
Brussels   Leipzig Breslau
Lille BELGIUM Cologne   Prague
Le Havre   Nuremberg
Paris Strasbourg   Vienna
Basle   Munich   Steyr   Budapest
ATLANTIC OCEAN   Nantes   Nevers SWITZERLAND   AUSTRO–HUNGARIAN EMPIRE
FRANCE   Lyon   Milan   Venice
Bordeaux   Turin Genoa   Belgrade
Santander   Toulouse Marseille   Florence   OTTOMAN EMPIRE
Oviedo   Bilbao   PAPAL STATES
Oporto   Corsica   Rome
SPAIN   Barcelona   Naples
PORTUGAL   Madrid   SARDINIA   KINGDOM OF THE TWO SICILIES
Lisbon   Valencia   Palermo
Balearic Is.   Sicily
Mediterranean Sea
Cádiz   Málaga

TIMELINE
1790–1800

1791 The U.S. Bill of Rights is ratified as the first 10 amendments to the Constitution.

1793 Eli Whitney develops the cotton gin, a mechnical device for removing seeds from cotton.

1793 French king Louis XVI is guillotined by revolutionaries in Paris.

1790   1792   1794

KEY:

Europe

Americas

Asia, Africa, and Oceania

1790 Benjamin Franklin dies, having invented bifocal glasses in the last year of his life.

1792 France becomes a republic and goes to war against Prussia and Austria.

1795 Russia, Prussia, and Austria partition (or divide) Poland; it will not become independent again until 1919.

↑ The *Great Eastern* was so large that it could carry 4,000 passengers.

Isambard Kingdom Brunel

Isambard Kingdom Brunel was the greatest engineer of the industrial age. He made his name in the 1830s, building England's Great Western Railway. To carry the track, he devised bridges that earned him a reputation for technical brilliance. Brunel then built iron steamships that revolutionized sea travel, culminating in the *Great Eastern*. The ship was an engineering triumph but a commercial failure. Exhausted, Brunel died in 1859, just a year after its launch.

Matthew Boulton, produced hundreds of efficient rotary motion engines to drive machinery in factories and mines.

Steam for Transportation

The next step was to apply steam to locomotion. Britain's extensive canal system struggled to carry the growing flow of raw materials and goods. The first steam railroad was built to carry coal from a mine to a waterway in northeastern England in 1825. Within decades the network had expanded greatly, carrying freight and passengers at previously unimagined speeds.

1795 Scottish explorer Mungo Park explores the course of the Niger River in central Africa.

1796 British doctor Edward Jenner develops a vaccination against smallpox.

1799 Napoleon Bonaparte makes himself first consul of France—effectively the nation's ruler.

1799 Eli Whitney uses an assembly line to mass-produce muskets for the U.S. Army.

1796   1798   1800

1796 John Adams is elected second president of the United States.

1798 French forces led by Napoleon Bonaparte occupy Egypt but are defeated by the British at the Battle of the Nile.

1799 The Dutch East Indies Company goes bust; its possessions in Southeast Asia become colonies of the Dutch state.

Timeline (continued)

1862 A machine gun is developed by U.S. inventor Richard Gatling; 25 years later, Hiram Maxim's version comes into widespread service.

1879 Thomas Alva Edison in the United States and Joseph Swan in England independently develop the electric light; Edison builds power plants to provide electric lighting for homes.

1885 German engineers Gottlieb Daimler and Karl Benz devise the internal combustion engine and build vehicles powered by it.

1903 Orville and Wilbur Wright undertake the first succesful powered flight of a heavier-than-air machine at Kitty Hawk, North Carolina.

« Brunel designed this double tunnel beneath the Thames River in London.

Britain's industrial monopoly was broken early in the nineteenth century. Belgium and France developed their textile, coal, iron, and arms industries. In Germany, industrialization began from the 1840s on. Growth accelerated after the unification of Germany in 1871. By 1900, Germany had overtaken Britain in steel production and led the world in making chemicals, including dyes, pharmaceuticals, and explosives. The United States started later than the European powers but experienced a spurt of growth in the decades following the Civil War that saw it quickly catch up.

Urbanization

The social impact of the Industrial Revolution was radical. The rural population of most of western Europe fell from 70 to under 10 percent between 1750 and 1914.

TIMELINE
1800–1810

1800 Italian physicist Alessandro Volta invents the first battery capable of storing electricity.

1801 French troops end their occupation of Egypt.

1804 Meriwether Lewis and William Clark set out on the first overland crossing to the Pacific and back; it will take two years.

1800   1802   1804

KEY:

- Europe
- Americas
- Asia, Africa, and Oceania

1801 Thomas Jefferson becomes U.S. president.

1803 With the Louisiana Purchase of land from France, the United States doubles its size.

1804 The English inventor Richard Trevithick designs the first self-propelling steam engine.

The new city dwellers experienced overcrowding, poor housing and health care, and periodic unemployment. Laws curbed the worst forms of exploitation, such as child labor and excessive hours. But by the end of the century, demands were growing for better political representation for working people. Labor unions and socialist parties were beginning to challenge the status quo.

Bessemer pioneered cheap steel. ⟫

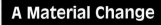

A Material Change

English inventor Henry Bessemer invented the process now named for him. The process used oxidation to convert iron into steel. The steel was produced in large quantities, and was strong and cheap. Steel soon began to replace iron. It enabled the building of large bridges, railroads, and buildings for which iron was too heavy.

⟪ Workers load coal into a furnace at an ironworks in 1835. Coal fueled industrial progress.

1805 French emperor Napoleon Bonaparte wins a decisive victory over the Austrians and Russians at the Battle of Austerlitz.

1807 Robert Fulton begins the world's first commercial steamboat service on the Hudson River in New York.

1809 Sweden hands Finland to Russia after being defeated in a brief war.

1806

1808

1810

1806 Congress authorizes the first federal highway, the Cumberland Road, although it is not begun until 1811.

1808 After Napoleon occupies Portugal and Spain, a British army lands in Portugal, beginning the six-year Peninsular War.

1810 Father Miguel Hidalgo leads an unsuccessful uprising in Mexico against Spanish rule.

The Beginning of Railroads

In early railroads, horses pulled wagons along wooden "roads." When much heavier steam locomotives replaced horses, the "iron road" was born.

This drawing shows the 1825 opening of the Stockton and Darlington Railway. →

TIMELINE
1810–1820

1812 The United States declares war on Great Britain, claiming that its trade is being hampered.

1812 Napoleon's army invades Russia and occupies Moscow; it is driven back by the harsh winter.

1814 The British burn Washington, D.C., ending the War of 1812.

1810

1812

1814

1811 King George III of England is declared insane; his son George becomes prince regent.

1811 Paraguay declares independence from Spain.

1814 Napoleon abdicates; the leaders of Europe meet at the Congress of Vienna to decide the continent's future.

KEY:

- Europe
- Americas
- Asia, Africa, and Oceania

The first steam locomotive was built in 1803 by English engineer Richard Trevithick. It ran along 10 miles (16 km) of cast-iron track in South Wales. The first railroad to carry passengers and freight opened in 1825: the Stockton and Darlington Railway. At first, passengers traveled in horse-drawn coaches, and only freight was steam hauled. The first intercity line opened in 1830 to carry cotton from the port of Liverpool to the mills in Manchester. The first train was hauled by Stephenson's *Rocket*.

Spread of Railroads

Railroads also sprang up in other countries. The year 1830 saw the inauguration of the Baltimore and Ohio Railroad. To operate it, American engineer Peter Cooper built

↞ This picture shows early locomotive designs, including the *Rocket* (bottom).

↓ Stephenson's *Rocket* was the most famous of the early engines.

Timeline of Early Railroads

1803 Richard Trevithick builds the first steam locomotive.

1825 Opening of the Stockton and Darlington Railway.

1830 The intercity Liverpool and Manchester Railway opens in northern England.

1830 The first railroad in the United States, the Baltimore and Ohio, opens.

1831 The South Carolina Railroad becomes the longest railroad (154 miles; 248 km) in the world.

1832 The first steam railroad opens in France.

1835 The first railroad opens in Germany.

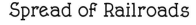

1815 Napoleon escapes from exile but is finally beaten at the Battle of Waterloo.

1816 French physician René Laënnec invents the stethoscope for listening to patients' hearts.

1818 The *Savannah* is the first steamship to sail the Atlantic.

1820 British settlers begin to arrive in great numbers in Cape Colony, southern Africa.

1816

1818

1820

1816 Argentina delcares its independence from Spain.

1816 Shaka becomes king of the Zulus and begins to expand Zulu power in southern Africa.

1819 Simón Bolivar frees Colombia from Spanish control.

Across America

Railroads played a vital part in bringing together the United States. Encouraged by a government act passed in 1862, a line was planned to link the eastern railroad network with California. Work began from the eastern and western ends of the new line. In the east, progress was more rapid over flatter land. In the west, work was harder and slower. The construction of tunnels and bridges through the Rockies was one of the great engineering feats of the time. The two lines met in Utah in May 1869.

Tom Thumb, the first steam locomotive to be made in the United States. The Philadelphia and Columbia Railroad opened with horse-drawn vehicles in 1831, but within three years, it had steam locomotives. The longest railroad in the world at the time, the South Carolina Railroad, also started operations in 1831. It ran for 154 miles (248 km) from Charleston to Hamburg.

In 1832, the first steam-hauled line in France opened between St. Étienne and Lyons; and in 1835, Germany's first railroad opened. By 1840, there were railroads in Austria, Ireland, and the Netherlands. As the new railroads appeared, canals fell into disrepair.

Railroad Equipment

The "road" of the original railroads employed iron rails. They were made of cast iron, at first with a right-angled section to keep the wheels on the track. Soon these flanged rails were replaced. The flanges were put on the wheels of the vehicles, which ran on short "fish-bellied" rails that were straight on top but curved beneath to make them thicker (and stronger) in the center. But

TIMELINE
1820–1830

1821 Greece begins a war of independence against the Ottoman Empire.

1822 Jean-François Champollion uses the Rosetta Stone to decipher ancient Egyptian hieroglyphics.

1823 In the Monroe Doctrine, U.S. president James Monroe recognizes the new countries of Latin America and warns against European interference in the region.

1820   1822   1824

KEY:

Europe

Americas

Asia, Africa, and Oceania

1821 Mexico wins independence from Spain.

1822 English mathematician Charles Babbage builds a prototype of his "difference engine," called the world's first computer.

1825 The world's first railroad, the Stockton and Darlington, opens in northern England.

The Liverpool and Manchester Railway mainly carried cotton to textile mills.

cast-iron rails were brittle and often broke. Beginning in 1858, they were replaced by steel rails, introduced by English steelmaker Henry Bessemer.

To enter sidings and branch lines, railroads need switches (known as "points" in Europe). They were invented in 1789 by English engineer William Jessop for tramways. The first signals took the form of disks or arms that rotated or pivoted like semaphore signals. In 1849, the New York and Erie Company introduced block signaling, which does not allow a train to enter a section of track until the previous train has left it. Soon block signals were linked electrically.

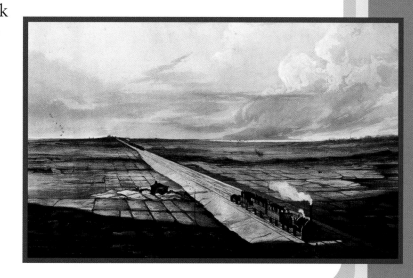

Early Views

Many people were wary about traveling on early railroads. The first passenger cars were open. Critics warned that passengers risked suffocating in the rushing air. The image of railroads was not helped by an incident at the opening of the Liverpool and Manchester Railway in 1830. The locomotive *Rocket* ran over a politician, who later died.

⇐ The Liverpool to Manchester line crossed a bog on hurdles driven into the wet ground.

1825 The 363-mile (584-km) Erie Canal opens, linking the Great Lakes with the Atlantic Ocean.

1827 The Baltimore and Ohio Railroad is chartered as the first commercial railroad to carry both passengers and freight.

1829 William Burt patents the first typewriter.

1826   1828   1830

1826 French inventor Joseph-Nicéphore Niepce takes the first permanent photograph.

1829 Turkey recognizes the Greeks' right to rule themselves (full independence is granted in 1832).

1830 Revolution in France forces Charles X to abdicate; he is replaced by the populist Louis Philippe.

The Great Exhibition

Staged in London in 1851, the first Great Exhibition was
a world's fair of exhibits designed to show the extent of
human achievement.

Paxton's design soon earned the nickname "Crystal Palace." ⇒

TIMELINE
1830–1840

1831 On board the *Beagle*, naturalist Charles Darwin makes discoveries that will lead to his theory of evolution.

1832 The Reform Act in Britain doubles the electorate to 1 million.

1835 U.S. inventor Samuel Colt patents his revolving-breech pistol ("revolver").

1830

1832

1834

1831 Nat Turner leads a slave revolt in Virginia.

1833 Britain passes a law abolishing slavery in its empire.

1834 Prussia forms the Zollverein, a customs union of German states that is an important step toward a unified Germany.

KEY:

Europe

Americas

Asia, Africa, and Oceania

Queen Victoria's husband, Prince Albert, became president of the Royal Society of Arts in 1843. Six years later, he came up with the idea of an exhibition to show off the "Industries of All Nations." At the time, industry was mainly concentrated in Britain. The country was sometimes known as "the workshop of the world."

A Glass Venue

Victoria herself was the first person to put up money for the project. Leading manufacturers also contributed to make up the £80,000 needed for a new building.

English architect Joseph Paxton received the commission to design a great building for Hyde Park, London. He designed a structure built entirely from prefabricated iron sections and glass. The Crystal Palace was "great" by any standards. It was 1,847 feet (563 m) long,

← Queen Victoria opens the Great Exhibition in London in 1851.

Timeline of International Exhibitions

1851 The Great Exhibition opens in London; more than half the exhibits come from Britain or its empire.

1853 The New York World's Trade Fair opens.

1855 The first Exposition Universelle is held in Paris (also 1867, 1878, 1889).

1873 Vienna stages the World's Fair.

1876 The Centennial Exposition in Philadelphia celebrates the 100th anniversary of the United States.

1893 The World's Columbian Exhibition in Chicago marks 400 years since Columbus landed in the Americas.

1835 In South Africa, 10,000 Boers (Dutch settlers) begin the Great Trek inland away from British control.

1838 The first railroad line opens in Russia between the czar's summer palace and St. Petersburg.

1839 A new sultan begins extensive reforms of the Ottoman Empire.

1840 An official report recommends the union of Upper and Lower Canada into a single country.

1836   1838   1840

1836 Texas wins independence from Mexico at the Battle of San Jacinto.

1838 Photography pioneers William Henry Fox-Talbot and Louis Daguerre make important breakthroughs in Britain and France, respectively.

1839 British troops occupy Hong Kong during tension over the import of opium to China.

World's Fair

The original Crystal Palace in Hyde Park was taken down in 1852. It was moved and rebuilt on a hill at Sydenham, a little south of London. There it remained in use for more than 80 years for exhibitions, shows, and other public events. In 1936, the building was destroyed by fire The name of Paxton's structure lives on today. The London district where it once stood is still known as Crystal Palace.

The interior of the Crystal Palace during an exhibition in 1861. ➔

↑ The Colt revolver was one of the many exhibits from the United States.

407 feet (124 m) wide, and over 100 feet (30.5 m) high. More than 3,000 iron columns and 2,000 girders supported 903,840 square feet (84,000 sq m) of glass—nearly enough to cover 17 football fields. The structure influenced the design of many later railroad stations in Europe.

On Display

About 14,000 exhibitors showed more than 100,000 examples of manufactured goods. They included everything from printing presses and locomotives to small items such as cutlery. The 560 exhibits from the United States included Cyrus McCormick's reaper and Samuel Colt's repeating revolver. The

TIMELINE
1840–1850

1842 Labor laws in Britain forbid women from working underground in coal mines.

1842 U.S. surgeon Crawford Williamson Long performs the first operation using anaesthetic (ether).

1844 U.S. inventor Samuel Morse sends the first telegraph message, from Washington to Baltimore.

1840   1842   1844

KEY:

Europe

Americas

Asia, Africa, and Oceania

1840 Britain and China start the First Opium War.

1845 Potato blight in Ireland causes famine that kills a million people and drives many more into exile.

French provided 1,700 exhibits. The exhibition was open for 23 weeks. It had more than 6 million visitors, most of whom got there by train. It also made a profit.

More Exhibitions

The Great Exhibition of 1851 was the first of several nineteenth-century international exhibitions in Europe and North America. Some were known as world's fairs rather than exhibitions. They all celebrated industrial and economic progress and technological

innovation. They took place in urban centers that were eager to promote themselves as capitals of progress, such as Vienna, Austria; Paris, France; and New York and Chicago in the United States. One of the grandest of the follow-up exhibitions was held in Chicago between May 1 and October 30, 1893. The 400th anniversary of the discovery of America was reflected in its title: the World's Columbian Exhibition.

World's Columbian Exposition

The 1893 Chicago exposition took place in a collection of 150 buildings known as the White City. With facades in the classical style, they were built as a so-called Court of Honor around a lagoon. A double row of columns led down to Lake Michigan. The style began the Beaux-Arts period of U.S. architecture that dominated city centers for the next 40 years.

↑ Poorer Londoners wait in line for cut-price entry to the 1851 exhibition.

1845 The United States annexes Texas.

1846 The United States goes to war with Mexico over the purchase of New Mexico.

1848 Prospectors swarm to the California gold rush.

1848 Prodemocracy uprisings sweep Europe amid calls for political change.

1846

1848

1850

1846 The U.S. Congress founds the Smithsonian Institution in Washington, D.C.

1848 The Mexican-American war ends; the United States gains all lands north of the Rio Grande.

1848 German political thinkers Karl Marx and Friedrich Engels write the *Communist Manifesto*, urging a workers' revolution.

Germs and Disease

In the nineteenth century, scientists realized that germs spread disease; they used new microscopes and techniques to track down the sometimes deadly microorganisms.

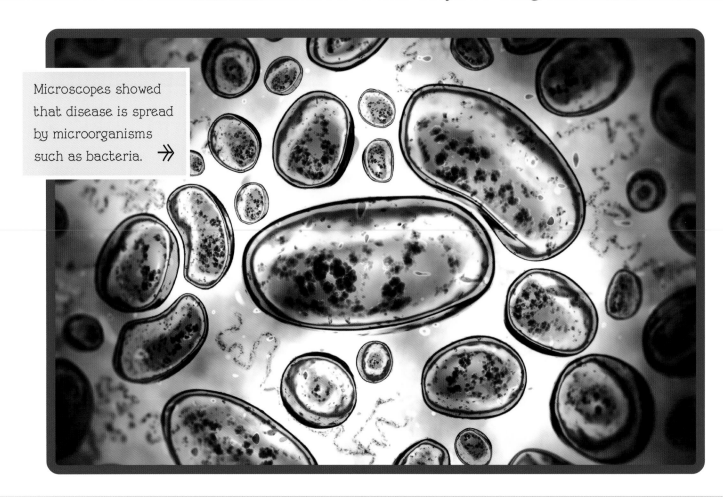

Microscopes showed that disease is spread by microorganisms such as bacteria. ⇒

TIMELINE
1850–1860

1851 In London, the Great Exhibition showcases the manufactured goods of an industrialized world.

1852 Harriet Beecher Stowe publishes the antislavery novel *Uncle Tom's Cabin*.

1853 A U.S. fleet arrives in Japan and forces Japan to make trade agreements.

1850   1852   1854

KEY:

Europe

Americas

Asia, Africa, and Oceania

1850 California joins the United States as the 31st state.

1851 U.S. inventor Isaac Singer patents the continuous-stitch sewing machine.

1854 The Kansas-Nebraska Act destroys the 1820 Missouri Compromise over slavery; it sparks heavy fighting in Kansas.

As early as 1546, Italian physician Girolamo Fracastoro suggested that germs cause disease. Nobody took much notice, even after 1676, when Dutch scientist Antonie van Leeuwenhoek first saw bacteria through a microscope. Then, in 1840, German Jacob Henle put forward the idea that infection is caused by parasitic organisms, the so-called germ theory of disease. The same theory was later also proposed by French chemist Louis Pasteur.

Bacteria

In 1877, German bacteriologist Robert Koch announced that staining bacteria made them easier to study. Danish physician Hans Gram used the idea to classify bacteria, which are now classed as either Gram-positive or Gram-negative. Bacteriologists also classify bacteria according to their shapes: coccus (round), bacillus (rod-shaped), spirochete (spiral), and so on.

Timeline of Germs and Disease

1546 Italian physician Girolamo Fracastoro suggests that germs cause disease.

1676 Antonie van Leeuwenhoek sees bacteria through his homemade microscope.

1840 German pathologist Jacob Henle's puts forward the germ theory of disease.

1882 Robert Koch discovers the bacterium that causes tuberculosis.

1884 Hans Gram uses stains to classify bacteria.

1897 Martinus Beijerinck discovers viruses, which are too small to be trapped in the same way as bacteria.

↑ Crowded, dirty cities were ideal places for germs to spread disease.

1856 British inventor Henry Bessemer invents a process (named after him) for making steel more efficiently and cheaply.

1857 U.S. inventor Elisha Otis installs the first safety elevator, in a building in New York City.

1860 Giuseppe Garibaldi and his Thousand Redshirts win control of Sicily and southern Italy as part of a campaign to create a united country.

1856   1858   1860

1855 Ferdinand de Lesseps wins the contract to build the Suez Canal in Egypt from the Mediterranean to the Red Sea.

1857 In India, a serious mutiny breaks out against British rule.

1860 The antislavery Abraham Lincoln is elected as 16th president of the United States.

Viruses

Nobody saw a virus until after the invention of the electron microscope in the 1930s. They turned out to have various shapes. Viruses cannot multiply outside a living cell; but once they force their way into a cell, they take it over and make it rapidly reproduce more virus particles. The particles break out and quickly invade other cells.

Viruses cause various diseases, such as HIV/AIDS (right). ⇑

The hunt was on. In 1880, German bacteriologist Karl Eberth found the bacillus that causes typhoid. In 1882, Robert Koch found the bacterium that causes tuberculosis, and German bacteriologists Friedrich Löffler and Wilhelm Schütz identified the cause of the animal disease glanders. In 1897, Danish veterinarian Bernhard Bang discovered a bacillus that causes abortion in cattle, and the Japanese bacteriologist Kiyoshi Shiga found the cause of endemic dysentery.

Other Causes of Disease

Bacteria are not the only parasitic microorganisms to cause diseases. Protozoans, for example, include the trypanosomes that cause sleeping sickness and Chagas' disease, the amebas that result in amebic dysentery, and the plasmodium parasite responsible for malaria.

Louis Pasteur used animals to test his first vaccines. ⇒

TIMELINE
1860–1870

1861 The American Civil War begins when Confederate forces shell Fort Sumter, South Carolina.

1863 Abraham Lincoln's Emancipation Proclamation declares that slaves living in the rebel states are free.

1864 Louis Pasteur introduces the process of pasteurization.

1860   1862   1864

KEY:

- Europe
- Americas
- Asia, Africa, and Oceania

1861 The Kingdom of Italy is proclaimed.

1861 Czar Alexander II emancipates (frees) Russia's serfs.

1865 The first transatlantic telegraph cable is laid.

← Bacteria come in many different sizes and shapes.

Some microscopic fungi produce diseases that affect the skin or lungs. Most of these microorganisms were tracked down by nineteenth-century microbiologists.

Bacteria and Viruses

In 1897, Dutch microbiologist Martinus Beijerinck showed that the microorganism that causes tobacco mosaic disease escapes through a filter that normally traps bacteria. He had discovered a new kind of microorganism: the first virus. A year later, the virus that causes foot-and-mouth disease in cattle was discovered. Since then, viruses have been found to be responsible for many diseases in humans, including yellow fever, influenza, polio, measles, and AIDS (acquired immune deficiency syndrome).

Almost as fast as bacteriologists found the bacteria that cause diseases, they developed vaccines against them, so that people could be injected and gain immunity. Vaccines for virus diseases proved more difficult but now exist for all the disorders named above except AIDS.

Louis Pasteur

Louis Pasteur helped popularize the germ theory of disease. In 1862, he used heat to kill microorganisms in liquids such as milk. This is called pasteurization. In the 1870s, Pasteur discovered how to make vaccines. He learned to inject a patient with a weak form of a disease. The patient's body fought off the disease. In doing so, it developed an immunity against the full disease.

← Robert Koch, like Pasteur, was a founder of modern bacteriology.

1865 The Confederates surrender, ending the American Civil War.

1867 The United States buys Alaska from Russia.

1868 The Fourteenth Amendment grants citizenship to former slaves.

1868 A revolution in Spain establishes constitutional monarchy.

1870 Prussian forces defeat France in the Franco-Prussian War.

1866

1868

1870

1865 President Abraham Lincoln is assassinated.

1867 The Dominion of Canada is created.

1869 The transcontinental railroad is completed when two lines meet at Promontory Point, Utah.

1869 The Suez Canal opens in Egypt.

The Age of Invention

The lives of ordinary people in the West were transformed
more radically by technology in the nineteenth century
than they had been in the preceding thousand years.

An early car made by
Karl Benz in 1895
draws curious looks
from spectators. ⟹

TIMELINE
1870–1880

1871 Reporter Henry
Morton Stanley tracks
down explorer David
Livingstone in east Africa.

1874 The Impressionist
group of artists hold their
first exhibition in France.

1874 Remington
introduces the first
commercial typewriter
in the United States.

1870   1872   1874

KEY:

Europe

Americas

Asia, Africa,
and Oceania

1871 Germany is
unified under Emperor
William I of Prussia.

1873 In India, the British Raj is
reformed to give local people
more say in government.

1875 Britain buys the
controlling share of
the Suez Canal.

↑ Michael Faraday pioneered electric motors.

The nineteenth century saw science come out of laboratories and technology emerge from the mills and mines. Just as steam power revolutionized industry early in the century, so electric power did the same later for everyday life. Electricity was at first little more than a scientific curiosity, its properties demonstrated to wondering gentlefolk at fashionable public lectures. In time, however, its practical applications began to be explored, a process in which British scientist Michael Faraday's discoveries were to prove far-reaching. His work on electromagnetism led to the invention of the electric motor and the transformer, complementary mechanisms from which many later developments would flow.

As the century went on, technological progress developed momentum as fresh inventors built on

Timeline of the Age of Invention

1804 Englishman Richard Trevithick invents a working steam locomotive.

1821 British scientist Michael Faraday invents the electric motor.

1831 Faraday develops the electric transformer and dynamo.

1832 U.S. painter Samuel Morse starts work on the electric telegraph; the first telegraph line is established in 1844.

1834 Jacob Perkins invents a refrigerator.

1845 U.S. inventor Elias Howe creates the first successful domestic sewing machine.

HOWE'S SEWING MACHINE.

↞ Howe's sewing machine was not the first, but it was very successful.

1876 Alexander Graham Bell patents the telephone.

1877 Thomas Alva Edison develops the phonograph for playing recorded music.

1877 Britain's Queen Victoria becomes Empress of India.

1880 Boers in the Transvaal declare independence from Britain, starting the First Boer War.

1876   1878   1880

1876 The Sioux defeat General Custer's U.S. forces at the Battle of the Little Big Horn.

1876 German composer Richard Wagner completes his Ring cycle of operas.

1879 In the Zulu War in South Africa, British forces are crushed at Isandhlwana.

Timeline (continued)

1858 Hamilton Smith devises the first rotary washing machine.

1876 Alexander Graham Bell invents the telephone.

1877 German engineer Niklaus Otto invents what is seen as the prototype for all later internal combustion engines.

1879 Thomas Edison captures the world's first recorded sound on his phonograph.

1885 Working independently, German engineers Karl Benz and Gottlieb Daimler develop the first functional automobiles.

1889 John Boyd Dunlop develops a successful pneumatic tire.

1898 Rudolf Diesel produces the engine that will be named after him.

↑ Samuel Morse invented his famous code for the electric telegraph.

the work of their predecessors. For example, France's Louis Thimmonier developed the first-ever sewing machine in 1830, but it was left to the American inventor Elias Howe to devise the first practical model for domestic use 15 years later. Samuel Morse conceived the idea of the telegraph in 1832. He and other pioneers then worked on the concept for the next 12 years, producing a series of refinements to improve the system. By 1866, a telegraph cable had been laid across the Atlantic Ocean.

Changing Everyday Life

Thomas Edison produced the first practical lightbulb in 1879, although other inventors had produced earlier experimental models. The Scots-born inventor Alexander Graham Bell is credited with the invention of the telephone, although refinements made by Edison were essential to the finished product. They included a vibrating microphone inside the mouthpiece.

TIMELINE
1880–1890

1881 The reformist Russian czar Alexander II is assassinated by revolutionaries.

1882 Britain occupies Egypt at the invitation of the Ottoman governor.

1884 At the Berlin Conference, European powers divide Africa into spheres of influence.

1880   1882   1884

KEY:

Europe

Americas

Asia, Africa, and Oceania

1881 U.S. president James Garfield is assassinated after less than a year in the post.

1882 New laws greatly restrict Chinese immigration to the United States.

1885 Leopold II of Belgium becomes ruler of the Congo Free State; millions of Africans will die under his rule.

railway network 1850
railways built 1850–70

0   600 km
0   400 mi

St. Petersburg
Gävle   Helsingfors
Christiania   Stockholm
Pskov
Inverness   Göteborg   Riga
North   Baltic
Glasgow Edinburgh   Sea   Sea
Belfast Darlington   Copenhagen Malmö   Königsberg
Stockton   Kiel   Danzig
Dublin   Manchester   Hamburg
Liverpool Birmingham   Bremen   Hanover Berlin Poznan Warsaw
Cardiff   Amsterdam   Breslau
London   Dortmund Leipzig
Brussels   Cologne   Prague   Lemberg
Le Havre   Frankfurt   Krakow
Paris   Reims   Nuremberg
ATLANTIC   Orléans   Strasbourg Munich Vienna
OCEAN   Tours   Basel   Budapest
Nantes   Zürich
Limoges   Geneva   Milan   Trieste
Bordeaux   Lyon   Turin   Venice Belgrade Bucharest
Toulouse   Genoa
Santander   Marseille   Florence   Sofia
León Bilbao   Corsica   Rome
Oporto   Zaragoza   Bari
Madrid   Barcelona   Naples
Lisbon   Valencia   Sardinia
Córdoba   Alicante   Palermo   Messina
Cádiz Málaga Cartagena   Mediterranean   Catania
Sea   Sicily

↑ The railroad era saw most of Europe crisscrossed with track by 1870.

Stephenson's Rocket

Stephenson's Rocket

On September 15, 1830, the world's first regular rail service opened between Manchester and Liverpool. The day was a triumph for the *Rocket*, the locomotive devised by British engineer George Stephenson that powered the train. Chosen against stiff opposition at the previous year's Rainhill Trials, it raced along, cheered by huge crowds.

← The *Rocket* was the most successful of a number of early steam locomotives.

Cumulatively, the breakthroughs by individuals of genius made the nineteenth century the age of invention: By its later decades, their discoveries were transforming the conditions of daily life. The first ether-based refrigerator was made by Jacob Perkins in 1834; by the end of the century,

1885 German engineers Gottlieb Daimler and Karl Benz both produce working motor cars.

1886 Apache chief Geronimo surrenders to U.S. forces.

1889 Scottish inventor John Dunlop invents the pneumatic tire.

1886   1888   1890

1886 The Statue of Liberty, a gift from France, is dedicated in New York City.

1888 The Young Turk movement is founded in Turkey to oppose the Ottoman Empire.

1889 The Eiffel Tower opens in Paris, France.

The Effect of Inventions

Inventions were not simply technological advances. They had implications for most areas of life. The railroad, for example, allowed bulk transportation and mass tourism. In turn, those developments brought changes in economic and cultural life. New transportation and communications also altered how people thought. They changed people's sense not just of space and distance but also of social geography, or how people saw other sections of society.

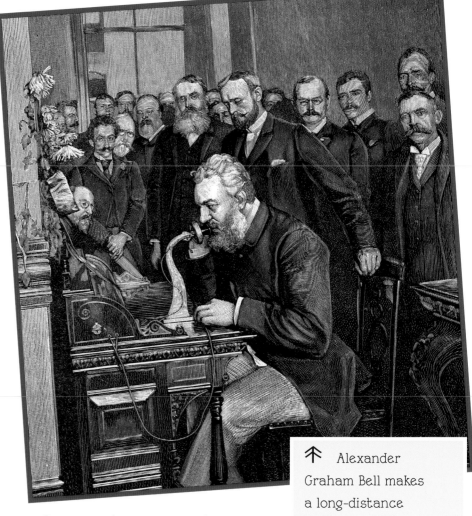

↑ Alexander Graham Bell makes a long-distance telephone call in 1892.

refrigerated storage and transportation were a fact of life. Charles Goodyear's discovery of "vulcanized" rubber (made more resilient by cooking it with sulfur) meant relatively little to the general public in 1839. It became far better known once John Boyd Dunlop made

TIMELINE
1890–1900

KEY:

Europe

Americas

Asia, Africa, and Oceania

1892 A violent strike breaks out at the Homestead Steelworks in Pittsburgh; the strikers are eventually defeated.

1893 The socialist Independent Labour Party is founded in Britain.

1890

1892

1894

1890 Sioux refugees are massacred by U.S. cavalry at Wounded Knee in South Dakota.

1893 The U.S. economy enters a four-year depression after railroad companies fail.

1893 A scandal over Jewish army officer Alfred Dreyfus splits France.

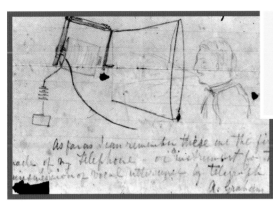

⇐ This sketch by Alexander Graham Bell shows an early idea for a telephone.

a practical pneumatic tire in 1889. In turn, Dunlop's discovery would only come into its own once the motor industry was born by a similar gradual process of improvement.

A Changed Continent

By 1900, railroads had shrunk traveling times hugely: It took days rather than weeks or months to cross the United States. Messages could be sent between continents by telegraph, people could speak by telephone from one city to another, sound had been recorded, and electricity illuminated workplaces and homes. Automobiles were becoming faster and more available, and the Wright Brothers were already thinking about the next great leap forward: flight.

American Genius

Thomas Alva Edison was one of the most influential inventors in history. Among his inventions that shaped the modern world were the lightbulb, the phonograph, and the movie camera. At his laboratories at Menlo Park, New Jersey, Edison brought together invention and industry. He used teams of inventors to develop and mass-manufacture devices for sale to ordinary Americans.

⇐ Edison's phonograph stored sounds on a wax cylinder.

1895 In France, the Lumière brothers show the world's first movie.

1897 English physicist Joseph Thomson discovers the electron.

1898 At the end of the war, Cuba becomes independent; the United States gains colonies in Puerto Rico, Guam, and the Philippines.

1896   1898   1900

1896 The U.S. Supreme Court rules that racial segregation is legal.

1898 An explosion on the USS *Maine* in Havana, Cuba, gives the United States a reason to begin the Spanish-American War.

1898 In France, Marie Curie and her husband Pierre discover radium.

Glossary

bacteria A type of single-celled microorganism that is found in almost every environment on earth, including the human body. Most bacteria are harmless to humans, but some cause diseases that can be fatal.

despot A ruler who holds absolute power and authority.

furnace A device used to heat substances to extreme temperatures, commonly used in the manufacturing of ceramics, the extraction of metal from ores, and metal casting.

loch A large body of water. In Scotland the word is used to describe lakes, estuaries, and fjords.

lock A system of gates that allow boats to be raised and lowered between stretches of water at different levels.

locomotive A locomotive is a railroad vehicle that provides the power to move a train. They can be powered by steam, electric or diesel engines.

mechanization Using machines to perform tasks previously done by humans or animals.

mill A factory in which many of spinning or weaving machines were installed. It was also used as a general term for a factory.

pharmaceuticals Chemical substances used in the treatment or prevention of disease.

philosopher A person who studies subjects such as ethics, human relationships, and the nature of thought and reality.

sluice A type of gate used to regulate the flow of water through a channel or river.

spindle A stick with tapered ends around which fibres from a raw material such as wool or cotton are twisted to make yarn.

traction engine A self-propelled mobile steam engine that was typically used as a portable source of power for agricultural machinery.

treadle A mechanism that allows a person to operate or power some functions of a machine with their feet.

vaccine A preparation that increases a person's immunity to specific diseases. A vaccine typically contains a trace amount of the microorganism that causes a disease, allowing a person's immune system to learn how to recognize and destroy it without putting them at risk of infection.

Further Reading

Books

Auerbach, Jeffrey A., and Peter H. Hoffenberg. *Britain, the Empire, and the World at the Great Exhibition of 1851.* Burlington, VT: Ashgate, 2008.

Bernstein, Peter L. *Wedding of the Waters: The Erie Canal and the Making of a Great Nation.* New York: W. W. Norton, 2006.

Dulken, Stephen. *Inventing the 19th Century: 100 Inventions that Shaped the Victorian Age, From Aspirin to the Zeppelin.* New York: NYU Press, 2006.

Garver, Thomas H. *The Last Steam Railroad in America.* New York: Harry N. Abrams, 2000.

Goodman, Deena, and Kathleen Wellman. *The Enlightenment.* Boston: Wadsworth Publishing, 2003.

Harrison, Mark. *Disease and the Modern World: 1500 to the Present Day.* Cambridge, MA.: Polity, 2004.

Leapman, Michael. *The World for a Shilling: How the Great Exhibition of 1851 Shaped a Nation.* London: Headline Book Publishing, 2002.

Marsden, Ben. *Watt's Perfect Engine: Steam and the Age of Invention.* New York: Columbia University Press, 2004.

Olson, James S. *Encyclopedia of the Industrial Revolution in America.* Westport, CT: Greenwood Press, 2001.

Price, Sean Stewart. *Smokestacks and Spinning Jennys: Industrial Revolution.* Chicago: Heinemann-Raintree, 2007.

Wiatrowski, Claude. *Railroads Across North America: An Illustrated History.* St. Paul, MN: Voyageur Press, 2007.

Web Sites

www.saburchill.com/history/chapters/IR/001.html
Information and images about the Industrial Revolution and its effects on Europe

www.bbc.co.uk/history/british/victorians
BBC website about the industrial revolution in Britain.

http://americanhistory.about.com/od/industrialrev/Industrial_Revolution.htm
Information about the Industrial Revolution and its effect upon America

Index

American Revolution 9
Baltimore and Ohio
    Railroad 29–30
Bell, Alexander Graham
    42, **44**, 45
Benz, Karl **40**
Bessemer, Henry 27, **27,**
    31
Bridgewater Canal 19, **19**
Brunel, Isambard
    Kingdom 25, **26**
canals 18–21, 25
    for irrigation 19
    in North America 21
    locks 20, **20**, 21, **21**
Coalbrookedale iron
    bridge, England **22**
Colt revolver 34, **34**
Crystal Palace **32**, 33–34,
    34
Deere, John 15
Encyclopedia, the
    9, **9**
enlightenment, the 6–9
    deism and 7–8
    empiricism and 8
    social reform and 8–9
Erie Canal 21
*Essay Concerning Human
    Understanding, An* 7
Faraday, Michael 41, **41**
farm machinery 14–17
    harvest machines
        16–17, **16**, **17**
    seed drill **15**, 16
    steam tractor 15, 17

Fench Revolution 9
Frederick the Great of
    Prussia **6**, 9
germs and disease 36–39
    bacteria 37–39, **39**
    microscopes and **36**, 37
    protozoans 38–39
    vaccines 39
    viruses 38, **38**, 39
Goodyear, Charles 44
Gram, Hans 37
Great Exhibition, the 17,
    32–35
        items on display 34–35
        subsequent
        exhibitions 35
Great Eastern 25, **25**
industrialization
    22–27, **24**
    child labor and **23**
    railroads and 25–26
    steam power and
        24–26
    the textile industry
        and 23
inventions and inventors
    40–45
    social impact of 44, 45
Koch, Robert 37, 38, **39**
lightbulbs 42
Linnaeus, Carolus **7**
Liverpool and Manchester
    Railroad 31, **31**
Locke, John 7
McCormick, Cyrus
    16–17, 34

mechanization 22, 23
    farming and 14–17
    harvesting and 16–17
    spinning and **10,**
        11–12, **11**
    weaving and 13
Morse, Samuel 42
New Lanark, Scotland **13**
Pasteur, Louis 37, **38**, 39
railroads 4, 25, 28–31, **43**
    public opinion and 31
    rail manufacture 30–31
Rocket 29, **29**, 31, 43, **43**
sewing machine **41**, 42
spinning machines **10**, **11**
Stockton and Darlington
    Railway **28**, 29
telegraph 42, **42**
telephones 42, **44**
textile machines 10–13,
    23
    loom 12–13, **13**
    spinning wheel 11, **11**
    spinning Jenny 12
Tom Thumb 30
Trevithick, Richard 29
Tull, Jethro 16
Voltaire **7**, **8**, 9
vulcanization 44–45
Watt, James 21, **23**, 24–25
weaving 12–13, **12**
World's Columbian
    Exhibition 35